MY FAVORITE FOODS

by Pearl Markovics

Consultant:
Beth Gambro
Reading Specialist
Yorkville, Illinois

Contents

My Favorite Foods 2

Key Words 16

Index..................... 16

About the Author 16

New York, New York

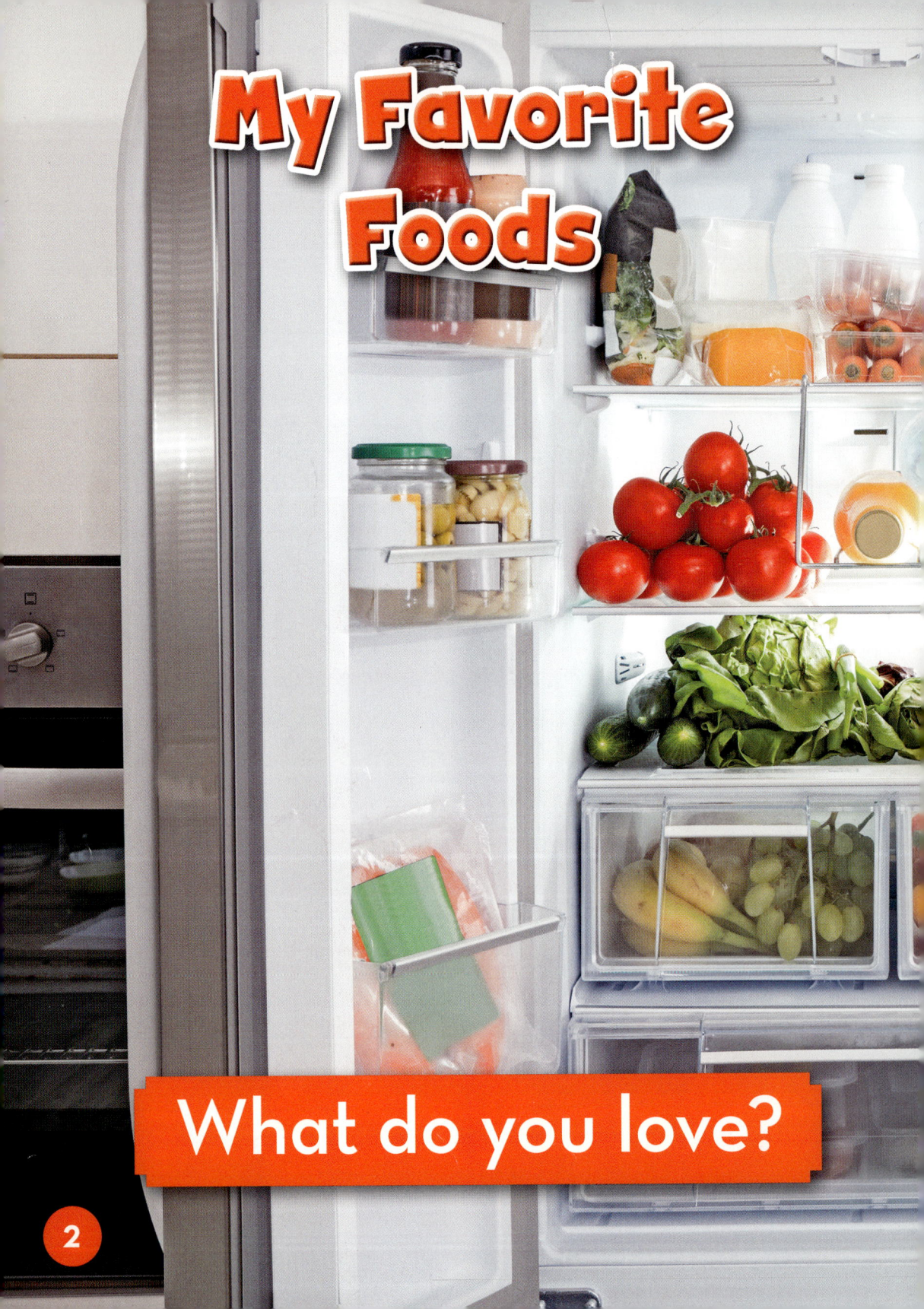

My Favorite Foods

What do you love?

I love food!

I love apples.

They are crispy.

I love pretzels.

They are crunchy.

I love popcorn.

It is salty.

I love strawberries.

They are sweet.

I love ice cream.

What food do you love?

Key Words

apples

ice cream

popcorn

pretzels

strawberries

Index

apples 4–5
ice cream 12–13

popcorn 8–9
pretzels 6–7

strawberries 10–11

About the Author

Pearl Markovics has many favorite things. She loves ice cream, especially when it's made from sheep's milk!